LET THE ZEPPELINS COME

To Barry

David Marks

Up ship!

David Marks

April 2017.

AMBERLEY

First published 2017

Amberley Publishing
The Hill, Stroud,
Gloucestershire, GL5 4EP

www.amberley-books.com

ISBN: 978 1 4456 6702 7 (print)
ISBN: 978 1 4456 6703 4 (ebook)

British Library Cataloguing in Publication Data.
A catalogue record for this book is available from the British Library.

Typeset in 10pt on 13pt Celeste.
Typesetting by Amberley Publishing.
Printed in the UK.

Contents

About this Book

I have collected First World War postcards for many years, starting with the official *Daily Mail* War Pictures, depicting scenes of the Battle of the Somme. Postcards of British generals and admirals soon followed, and among them was an image of a youthful lieutenant in a simple uniform, a stark contrast to the rows of medals and regalia worn by the venerable military leaders. The young man's name was William Leefe Robinson, and he was a Victoria Cross winner, who had 'attacked an enemy airship under circumstances of great difficulty and danger, and sent it crashing to the ground as a flaming wreck'. This card began my fascination with Germany's aerial bombing campaign against Britain and, as I researched the subject, the role of Robinson and his fellow pilots loomed large in the story of how the seemingly invincible Zeppelin was defeated.

I quickly discovered that a huge variety of postcards were published relating to Zeppelin raids. There were striking images of airships caught in the beams of searchlights or falling in flames, as well as the wrecks themselves. Robinson was there too, now clearly identifiable in a Royal Flying Corps Maternity Pattern Service Dress Jacket and with a ready smile. He was joined by his fellow pilots, who had also dealt the fatal blows against the 'Baby Killers', as the Zeppelins became known.

Postcards of the damage caused by the raids were quickly produced and circulated in the early months of the campaign, before the government began to censor such output. There were also images of large groups of soldiers and civilians, young and old, standing amid the devastated ruins of their towns and villages, or posing in bomb craters or with the bombs themselves. Powered flight was still in its infancy, as Louis Blériot had only crossed the English Channel in 1909, so what must have these people been thinking? Giant airships, well over 500 feet in length, had hovered overhead at the dead of night and dropped bombs with impunity. It must have been a truly frightening experience.

However, another sort of postcard began to emerge almost immediately the raids began. Comic postcards were being produced in great numbers by talented artists, as publishers quickly moved to reflect the many challenges to the everyday lives of the public. This book puts these postcards into context with the wider story of the 'First Blitz', demonstrating how they were used to boost the public's morale and to create a collective resolve. Comic postcards reinforced the belief that Britons everywhere could cope and, eventually, conquer the Zeppelin threat. The humour was good natured and simple, in contrast to the underlying vindictiveness often seen in French and German postcards of the time.

Everything illustrated in this book is from my own collection, at the heart of which is my archive of postcards; if a particular area or theme is not represented, it is simply because I have been unable to acquire a postcard of it. I have resisted the temptation to draw on, for example, the photographic collections held by the Imperial War Museum or the RAF Museum, as what these fine collections and others often lack is the immediacy that a postcard can bring, capturing a moment in time to be shared and, as you will see, in many instances carrying a pertinent message direct from the writer.

In September 1916, once the defending aircraft were equipped with the right ammunition to bring down the raiders, the tone of the comic postcards became triumphant. This was also reflected in the public's insatiable desire for relics as crowds descended on the crash sites in their thousands.

I have also included examples of how the postcard was used as a propaganda tool in Germany, with the authorities promoting its remarkable technology as a weapon of war. I will also introduce the reader to another aspect of the public's stoicism against the aerial threat – namely the production and sale of souvenir china. Never in the wildest dreams of the German High Command could they have considered that the British public would be buying china models for their mantelpieces depicting the Zeppelins themselves and the bombs that had destroyed property and claimed lives.

Once the threat from the air passed from the Zeppelin to the aeroplane, in the guise of the Gotha bomber and Staaken 'Giant' R-plane, postcards produced by both sides virtually disappeared and, in the closing chapter, I shall briefly consider the impact of this aspect of the air war.

While the key events of the First Blitz are covered in this book, it is not intended to be a 'raid by raid' account. My library contains numerous well-thumbed volumes, which have been published over the course of the last ninety years or so and tell the story in extensive detail. Some concentrate on specific geographical areas, such as London, and others serve as a general narrative on the raids as a whole. Nor is the book a technical publication; again, there are many quality publications setting out the specifications and performance of the various classes of Zeppelin. Personally, I can only marvel at the advances in aeronautical design carried out over a relatively short period of time by the Zeppelin Company and its contemporaries, and the bravery of the crews that flew them.

There are a number of books on First World War postcards but not, to my knowledge, a standalone volume on the Zeppelin raids, as portrayed through the postcards and other souvenirs of the day. This book is something a little different and also serves as a journey through my own collection, one that I hope readers will enjoy.

About the Author

David Marks lives and works in London. He is a member of the Airship Heritage Trust and a committee member of Cross & Cockade International (The First World War Aviation Historical Society). He regularly lectures on behalf these organisations on the subject of Zeppelin raids. He also writes Cross & Cockade's quarterly email newsletter, 'Wind in the Wires', which has over 1,100 subscribers, as well as contributing to journals and magazines.

In 2016, David was proud to be a member of the committee set up by the Northaw & Cuffley Parish Council to commemorate the centenary of the shooting down of airship SL11 by Lieutenant William Leefe Robinson.

David can be contacted via Twitter @ZeppRaider, where he would be delighted to discuss any aspect of First World War aviation.

7660 A   LIEUT. WILLIAM LEEFE ROBINSON. V.C.   ROTARY PHOTO. E.C.
"HE ATTACKED AN ENEMY AIRSHIP UNDER CIRCUMSTANCES OF GREAT DIFFICULTY
AND DANGER, AND SENT IT CRASHING TO THE GROUND AS A FLAMING WRECK."

Here is the postcard that inspired my interest in the Zeppelin raids. A youthful Leefe Robinson, pictured in the uniform of the 5th (Militia) Worcestershire Regiment.

THE END OF THE "BABY-KILLER."

Right: The image of a giant airship, caught in the beams of the searchlights and falling in flames, would stay in the memories of all who witnessed it for the rest of their lives.

Below: Following a Zeppelin raid on Lowestoft on the night of 15/16 April 1915, the Norfolk Regiment were on parade in a bomb crater in Denmark Road.

HOLE MADE BY ZEPPELIN BOMB IN DENMARK RD LOWESTOFT APRIL 1915

"HERE'S THE ZEPPELINS, BILLY— COME UNDER COVER!"

Left: Zeppelin raids stimulated a range of comic postcards such as this one, making light of a serious situation.

Below: German 'Future Music'. Published in Berlin in 1914, this propaganda postcard celebrates not only 'our' Zeppelin, but also the 'Big Bertha' super-heavy howitzer and the precision model rifle.

Please keep the Zepps away to-night,
Keep me safe till morning light;
And if you see the Kaiser bending,
Please put a bomb beneath his ending.
AMEN.

This little girl prays for a
Zeppelin-free night and suitable
punishment for the Kaiser, who is
depicted as a menacing 'Gas Bag'.

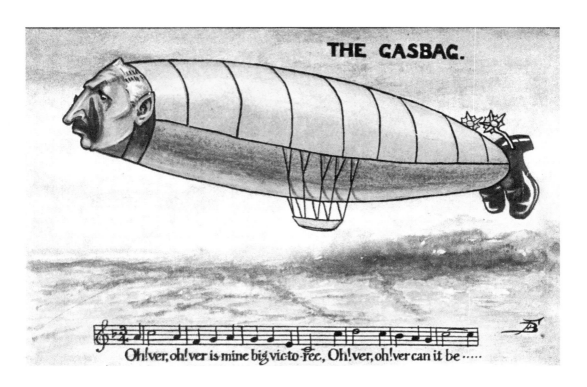

Introduction: A Brief History of the Zeppelin at War

Zeppelins had fired the imagination of the German people since the maiden flight of *LZ1* on 2 July 1900; they were a source of pride, fascination and wonder. Count Ferdinand von Zeppelin became the figurehead of a culture that embraced the technological advances of the day. After enduring numerous successes and failures, and with the continued support of the German people, the Zeppelin, together with the wooden-framed airships produced by rival manufacturer Schütte-Lanz, became an established part of Germany's Army and Naval Services.

In the years immediately preceding the First World War, the British authorities and the population at large had become increasingly concerned that the threat of a marauding fleet of airships would spearhead an invasion. The popular press exacerbated such fears, and there were 'phantom' airship scares in 1909 and 1912 with purported sightings over the British coast. When War was declared, it was believed that it would only be a matter of time before the might of the Zeppelins would be unleashed.

However, at the outbreak of the War, Germany possessed just eleven airships, and early offensive operations by Army airships revealed that they were extremely vulnerable to ground fire, unless flown at high altitude, and several were lost. However, the German public quickly clamoured for the Zeppelin to bring terror and panic to the streets, and to strike at the enemy's heart: London.

On the night of 19 January 1915, the first Zeppelin raid was successfully carried out, with Great Yarmouth, King's Lynn and surrounding villages being the first recipients of salvos of high explosive and incendiary bombs. From this relatively modest start, which killed four, the frequency of the raids increased, as more advanced and increasingly larger airships became operational.

By the end of 1915, there had been twenty raids on Britain, covering the length of the East Coast from Northumberland to Kent, which left over 200 dead and 500 injured. Significantly, London was bombed by a Zeppelin for the first time in May; there were a further four raids on the capital between August and October, taking place with increasing ferocity and loss of life. No aeroplanes appeared in opposition to the Zeppelins, which were able to steer an 'almost leisurely' course over London. Falling shrapnel from anti-aircraft shells caused more damage on the ground than in the air.

Home defences were seriously inadequate and questions were asked in Parliament. There were cries for retaliation, but this was not seriously considered until the development of aircraft with sufficient capacity and range, later in the conflict. The War Office and the Admiralty finally settled their differences as to how best to protect the capital and beyond; measures including improved guns, linked searchlight stations and co-ordinated aircraft squadrons began to challenge the raiders when hostilities resumed in 1916.

Behind the scenes, ways were being devised to defeat the Zeppelin. The problem was how to ignite the hydrogen gas that escaped from any tear in the gas cells created by a bullet's passage. Trials of explosive and phosphorus bullets were successfully carried out and, from July 1916, the machine gun drums of defending aircraft were routinely filled with a combination of this ammunition.

'God Punish England' reads the caption on this dramatic postcard, published by Josef Eberle for the German Schools Association.

A multi-image postcard showing scenes of the damage inflicted by *L3* on the St Peter's Plain area of Great Yarmouth.

The 'Midnight Assassin' sows death and destruction over the East Coast. Following a stricter implementation of the Defence of the Realm Act, official news of the raids was limited to the barest facts so as not to assist the German authorities.

The skeleton of 'super' Zeppelin *L33*. A 650-foot-long behemoth brought down on the night of 23/24 September 1916 by improved anti-aircraft defences.

Above left: Home defences left a lot to be desired in the early stages of the conflict.

Above right: Once armed with the latest incendiary ammunition, Royal Flying Corps aeroplanes had success after success over the Zeppelin.

Right: The disruption of a raid often resulted in the population having a 'Zeppelin Night', which could adversely affect productivity the following day.

The result was extraordinary and, on the night of 2/3 September 1916, a Schütte-Lanz airship was brought down over mainland Britain by Lieutenant William Leefe Robinson. As already mentioned, he was awarded the Victoria Cross for his exploits. This was swiftly followed by the destruction of three of the newest 'super' Zeppelins, which were 650 feet in length, over the following weeks.

The invincibility of the Zeppelins had been broken; when an aircraft armed with the new incendiary and explosive ammunition got an airship in its sights, it was inevitably doomed. Zeppelins had been unable to attack in sufficient numbers when home defences were at their weakest and failed to bring the country to its knees. While there were further sporadic raids into 1917 and 1918, the air raid initiative passed from airships to aeroplanes.

Airships made around fifty bombing raids on Britain during the war; official estimates list 557 people as being killed, including 498 civilians, and 1,358 injured. The casualty figures were minor in comparison with the daily returns from the Western Front. However, the Zeppelins accomplished one of their tactical objectives, causing vast disruption to wartime production every time a factory was blacked out in anticipation of a raid. Transport systems were also vulnerable, making the workforce late the morning after a raid. The efficiency of workers was also impaired by the impact of disrupted sleep from the night raids, as well as any false alarms.

Air raid precautions also meant that thousands of men manned the anti-aircraft guns and searchlights, observers dotted the countryside and trained aircraft squadrons had to be allocated to Home Defence duties. This diverted vital resources that might otherwise have been deployed on the Western Front. However, the Zeppelin raids intensified anti-German feeling and boosted recruitment.

The doctrine of bombing attacks on military and economic infrastructure behind the front lines, both as propaganda and as a means of diverting resources, eventually led to the modern-day concept of total war. In the following chapters, we can see how, through the medium of the humble picture postcard, this unprecedented development in warfare developed.

Chapter One:
'A Neighbourly Visit'

Antwerp had been bombed by a Zeppelin on 25/26 August 1914 and the German advance had also been aided by Zeppelin raids over the key fortified towns of Liege (known to the Germans as Lüttich) and Belfort. German postcard publishers were quick to demonstrate the might of this fearsome new weapon.

The War Office and the Admiralty were fully aware of the need to create and maintain an aerial defence of Britain, but neither could agree on how this should be done. Fortunately Winston Churchill, First Lord of the Admiralty since 1911, was at hand to set out a plan to combat the Zeppelin menace.

Initially, Churchill's typically aggressive policy resulted in aerial attacks on the Zeppelin sheds from forward bases at Antwerp, the most successful of which took place on 8 October 1914, when Flight Lieutenant Reginald Marix, flying a Sopwith Tabloid, caused the destruction of a Zeppelin in its shed at Düsseldorf. However, Antwerp fell into German hands two days later and the Royal Naval Air Service ('RNAS') had to select other targets in order to pursue Churchill's strategy.

There were six 'shed' raids in total during 1914 by the RNAS, including a daring raid on Friedrichshafen, the home of the Zeppelin Works, in November. During the attack, one of three raiding pilots narrowly missed destroying one of the latest Zeppelins.

The German press claimed that the first air raid on Britain was carried out by an Army 'taube' aircraft on 25 October 1914. However, British records do not mention the raid by *Leutnant* Karl Caspar and it is widely acknowledged that the first aerial bomb on Britain fell on 24 December 1914, courtesy of a seaplane, which landed in a Dover cabbage patch.

The following day, the RNAS and Royal Navy combined in an unsuccessful attempt to bomb the Zeppelin sheds at Nordholz, near Cuxhaven, using seaplanes housed on converted cross-channel steamers and supported by submarines. The British force was engaged by Zeppelins and defending seaplanes.

Rt. Hon. Winston Churchill.

Above left: In this patriotic postcard, Count Ferdinand von Zeppelin announces that he will be making a neighbourly visit to London from his new home at the Belgian city of Antwerp.

Above right: The message on the back of this early postcard reads: 'This is what you will find yourself like when you can't match your tie and socks.' The invasion threat, together with the Zeppelin raids and naval bombardments, were used as recruitment tools for the Army.

Left: Winston Churchill was thirty-nine years old on the outbreak of the First World War. 'The Power behind the Fleet' was also a great advocate of the use of aeroplanes in combat.

A piece of original art work by Archie Gilkison, described as the 'Wilfred Owen of cartooning'. His cartoons appeared regularly in newspapers such as the *Glasgow Herald* and *Evening Times* from 1914 to 1916. The 1914 'Story of the Zeppelin' nicely sums up British attitudes towards the perceived Zeppelin threat.

A dramatic depiction of the audacious RNAS raid on the Zeppelin airship sheds and factory at Friedrichshafen, penetrating 120 miles into Germany.

Der Flieger-Leutnant Caspar warf als erster in diesem Kriege Bomben auf Dover hinab.

German postcard publishers were quick to commemorate the 'first' aeroplane raid on the British mainland. A typically vivid image bearing little relation to the actual event!

Left: Some of the bomb shrapnel from the first raid on British soil was mounted and presented to King George V.

Right: For propaganda purposes, the Germans portrayed the Christmas Day clash between a Zeppelin and RNAS seaplanes as a major victory.

Chapter Two: 'Acts of the King's Enemies'

In January 1915, following sustained lobbying by his advisors, Kaiser Wilhelm II finally gave his qualified approval for the aerial bombardment of Britain, but excluding London.

An attempted raid on 13 January was abandoned, owing to heavy rain, but by 19 January conditions were favourable and on that fateful morning two Zeppelins of the German Naval Airship Division, *L3* and *L4*, left their sheds at Fühlsbüttel naval base just north of Hamburg. The commanders, Hans Fritz and Count Magnus von Platen-Hallermund, were given orders to attack dockyards and port installations along the shores of the Humber.

By 8.25 p.m., *L3* had arrived over the town of Great Yarmouth. Over the next ten minutes, the airship inflicted casualties by dropping its bombs from a height of 5,000 feet. The third bomb landed close to the town centre in St Peter's Plain, killing Samuel Alfred Smith, a fifty-three-year-old cobbler, and Martha Mary Taylor, a seventy-two year-old spinster. They were the first civilians killed by aerial bombardment in Great Britain.

A local doctor, Leonard Ley, recounted in his memoirs that 'later [that evening] I went to the Hospital, where a poor old lady had been brought in dead. I remember she wore a bonnet and a long "dolman cape". I turned it back and revealed all her intestines'.

By 11 p.m., after dropping bombs around West Norfolk and passing over the Sandringham Estate, *L4* reached King's Lynn. The third bomb to hit the town exploded with devastating effect in the congested Bentinck Street area. Percy Goate, aged fourteen, and a twenty-six-year-old war widow, Mrs Alice Maude Gazley, were killed. Following an inquest, their deaths were recorded as being 'from the effects of the acts of the King's Enemies'.

From the outset of the conflict, newspapers and periodicals began to offer financial assistance to subscribers who were victims of air raids and, as the flyer shown on p. 23 proclaims, twelve householders in Yarmouth benefited from the Zeppelin and Accident Insurance cover provided by the *Daily News*. An official scheme for insuring against damage due to aerial bombardment was introduced in July 1915, insuring against damage 'caused by aerial craft, or shots, shells, bombs or missiles from or used against aerial craft'.

10772-15   THE GERMAN AIR RAID ON GREAT YARMOUTH, JANUARY 19th, 1915.   ROTARY PHOTO. E.C.
DAMAGED HOUSES AT ST PETER'S PLAIN

Above: The aftermath of the bombing of St Peter's Plain, Great Yarmouth, where the first civilian fatalities of the War occurred. Can you spot the 'lucky' horseshoe on the ruined building?

Left: An explosive bomb struck the pavement at the back of 78 Crown Road, Great Yarmouth, but failed to explode. It was recovered and taken to the nearby Drill Hall and later defused.

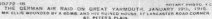

An explosion blew out the front of Mr Ellis's house, St Peter's Villa. He is pictured with his head swathed in bandages. Fortunately, Mrs Ellis and the rest of her family were on holiday in Cornwall.

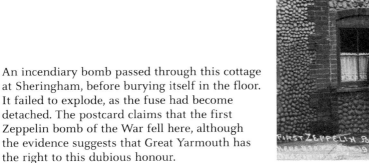

An incendiary bomb passed through this cottage at Sheringham, before burying itself in the floor. It failed to explode, as the fuse had become detached. The postcard claims that the first Zeppelin bomb of the War fell here, although the evidence suggests that Great Yarmouth has the right to this dubious honour.

Picking through the ruins of Bentinck Street, King's Lynn, where Alice Gazley and Percy Goate died. Mrs Gazley's husband had been killed in action just two months earlier, and Percy Goate's uncles, George and Richard, were both killed fighting on the Western Front later in the War.

This postcard shows the extensive damage to East Street, King's Lynn, with the local residents posing for the cameras.

ZEPPELIN BOMB DROPPED ON HEACHAM

Above: *L4* dropped two bombs over Heacham, one of which failed to explode and was found two days later. The bomb was displayed locally under guard until the following Sunday, with PC 78 Brookes keeping order.

Right: Throughout the War, newspapers offered their readers compensation for accidents and the effects of Zeppelin raids, underwritten by insurance companies.

ZEPPELIN
or Aeroplane
BOMBS

═══════════════

12 Householders in
YARMOUTH
HAD ALL DAMAGE FROM BOMBS PAID BY

The

𝔇𝔞𝔦𝔩𝔶 𝔑𝔢𝔴𝔰

═══════════════

HOW TO DO IT SEE OTHER SIDE.

ZEPPELIN AND ACCIDENT INSURANCE.

£10,000
FREE COMPENSATION FUND.

The Proprietors of "THE DAILY NEWS" will pay

£250

in the case of damage by Aerial Attack:

£25

in the case of damage by Bombardment from the Sea, or by our own Anti-Aircraft Guns.

The Ocean Accident and Guarantee Corporation, Limited,
(Empowered by Special Act of Parliament)
PRINCIPAL OFFICE: 36 to 44, Moorgate Street, London, E.C.

ACCIDENT.	WILL PAY
£1,000 (or £100 per annum for (15 Years)	to the legal personal representatives of the bona fide holder of this Coupon-Insurance Ticket if such holder shall be fatally injured by an accident within the United Kingdom to a passenger-train, passenger-steamer, public omnibus, tramcar, or cab (which is being driven by a licensed driver paying for public hire), in which such holder is at the time of such injury travelling as a ticket (or passbearing or fare paying passenger (or will pay to such holder should such accident cause non-fatal injury to such holder:
£1,000 (or £100 per annum for (15 years")	for the Loss of Two or more Limbs by actual separation at or above the wrist or ankle or of Both Eyes or the Loss of one or more Limbs as above defined, accompanied by the Loss of One or Both Eyes; OR
£500 (or £50 per annum for 15 years")	for the Loss of One Limb as above defined or One Eye only; OR
£1 10s. per week	during total disablement from earning a livelihood

* If such holder shall so long live.
Provided that the above undertaking is subject to the special conditions as published in "The Daily News," which are of the essence of the contract.

To obtain the above benefits the reader must order "The Daily News" from his newsagent and obtain from him this

---

FORM OF RECEIPT TO BE SIGNED BY NEWSAGENT AND RETAINED BY THE SUBSCRIBER.

I hereby acknowledge the receipt from

Subscriber's Signature ....

Address ....

this 6th day of March, 1915, of an order for the delivery to his address of one copy of "The Daily News" daily from this date until further notice and including the benefit of the Free Compensation Fund and Accident Benefits, subject to all the conditions specified in "The Daily News" from time to time.

Newsagent's Signature ....

Newsagent's Address ....

14. stamp to be affixed by subscriber to entitle to Compensation Fund.

IMPORTANT CONDITIONS :—(1) To render this receipt valid for the purpose of the Insurance, it is essential that "The Daily News" be delivered to the Subscriber daily at his address, and that this receipt be signed by Subscriber and the Newsagent prior to the accident. (2) When claiming, this receipt must be produced.

Newsagents, please note.—All that is requested of the newsagent is to sign the above receipt for the order given to him and to deliver "The Daily News" in accordance with the order. The house (if his own property, furniture, and household effects of every newsagent who regularly supplies "The Daily News" to customers will be covered subject to all conditions specified in "The Daily News" provided he stamps and signs the form above in favour of himself.

SEE OTHER SIDE.

This leaflet issued by the *Daily News* in March 1915 explains that it will pay out £250 in the case of damage by aerial attack.

Serie 33/3   Westl. Kriegsschauplatz, 20. Januar 1915: Angriffe deutscher Marineluftschiffe auf die engl. Ostküste.

A German postcard reveals the rudimentary bombing techniques employed by early Zeppelins, which had open gondolas. In the wake of international condemnation, the card subtly reinterprets the raid by depicting the attack as taking place on a fortified place.

Chapter Three: 'There's a Light that's Burning in the Window'

The Zeppelins returned in mid-April 1915 with a number of ineffectual raids over Eastern England. From Northumberland to Essex, the temptation to pose in a bomb crater or with the bombs themselves was irresistible, irrespective of the fear and anxiety that must have been felt.

With the world's first strategic bombing campaign now underway, lighting restrictions that had first been introduced in September 1914 were now being rigorously enforced. The Home Office issued its first memorandum on lighting in April 1915, which resulted in street lights being either unlit, dimmed or shaded. In homes, blinds and black-out curtains were used. Repeated failure to comply with the regulations resulted in cases being brought before the courts. Fines were generally around £5 and, given that the price of letter postage in 1915 was one penny, you can see how seriously this was taken.

While there was initially a great deal of disruption, with many minor accidents taking place, postcard publishers were quick to illustrate humorously how the regulations would impact on the public. A common theme was that of the drunken gent with the glare emanating from his reddened nose falling foul of the regulations. The population, particularly in towns and cities, soon adapted to the new regime.

Raids continued during the spring, as improved airships were brought into service, testing the limited home defences with the ultimate goal of reaching London. On 29/30 April, Suffolk was bombed by *LZ38*, the latest German Army Zeppelin, which was commanded by *Hauptmann* Erich Linnarz. A large concentration of high explosive and incendiary bombs were dropped on Bury St Edmunds, but there were no casualties.

The public were fascinated by the incendiary bombs, with their tar-covered rope, which helped prevent the dispersion of Benzol, tar and Thermite, as well as also being flammable. W. H. Goss, a leading maker of crested china – small, off-white china ornaments with a civic crest that were a popular keepsake for pre-war travellers – began to create designs relating to the conflict. Their models based on incendiary bombs recovered from Maldon and Bury St Edmunds were accurately portrayed and very popular.

On 10 May, *LZ38* returned to bomb Southend, while enduring heavy anti-aircraft fire. Little damage was caused, with just one fatality. The raid was fully reported in a special eighteen-page supplement to *The Southend Standard* with photographs and graphic accounts. Another local paper also printed a detailed account. In fact, the accounts were so detailed that they contravened the fairly mild guidelines previously published by the government under the Defence of the Realm Act 1914 and resulted in a D Notice being issued immediately afterwards, restricting the press from giving information that might be useful to the enemy.

Postcard publishers continued to raise the morale of the public, showing defiance and challenging the Zeppelins to attack. In reality, defences were still underprepared and, as the remainder of 1915 would demonstrate, things would need to improve significantly.

Left: 'Mind your nose doesn't show a light like the fair gents on the opposite side', is the message on this card, designed by Doug Tempest. Breaching the rules on lighting restrictions could result in heavy fines.

Above and Opposite below: A schoolboy stands in a crater created by a bomb dropped by *L9* on 14 April 1915 on Bedlington in the North East. In Reydon, one mile north-west of Southwold, Suffolk, the Snowling family had a narrow escape from the bombs of *L5* the following night.

Right: In Southwold itself, a dapper Cecil Robinson posed happily with the remains of the incendiary bomb he was able to put out.

Above left: The police regulations are on display as another red-nosed gent gets a warning.

Above right: 'Put out that blooming light!' shout the crowd as the Zeppelin hovers overhead.

Left: This little girl obeys the regulations and stays fashionable.

CARRYING OUT THE POLICE REGULATIONS
(Fitting Dark Blinds to her sitting room).

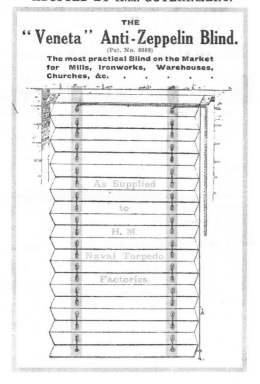

ADOPTED BY H.M. GOVERNMENT.

THE
" Veneta " Anti-Zeppelin Blind.
(Pat. No. 6869)

The most practical Blind on the Market
for Mills, Ironworks, Warehouses,
Churches, &c. . . . .

As Supplied

to

H. M.

Naval Torpedo

Factories.

Even the War
has its advantages

MÉME LA GUERRE A SES AVANTAGES.

Above left: The public needed to ensure that their homes or businesses were properly blacked-out. The makers of the 'Veneta' Anti-Zeppelin Blind advertise their successful product, which was used by factories and institutions across the country.

Above right: The chance of a romantic evening in the dimly lit streets was a potential benefit of reduced lighting, as demonstrated by prolific postcard artist Donald McGill. Note the shaded street lamp.

Right: These policemen are clearly undecided about whether to enforce the lighting regulations.

" Do you think there is too much light at that window ?"
" Oh ——I don't know !"

This postcard, posted on 8 May 1915, shows the damage inflicted on the Butter Market, Bury St Edmunds. The pile of rubble is the boot-maker's shop owned by Jeremiah Day at No. 32.

This widely distributed postcard shows at least forty-one of the incendiaries that fell on Bury St Edmunds.

Above: Here are some examples of crested china Zeppelin incendiary bombs produced by (from left to right) Arcadian, Grafton, Shelley and W. H. Goss. The Bury St Edmunds bombs were the template for these popular souvenirs.

Right: The Maldon incendiary bomb was of a cylindrical or 'Goldschmidt' type.

GERMAN INCENDIARY BOMB. WEIGHT ABOUT 16 lbs.
DROPPED AT MALDON DURING AIR RAID APRIL 16/15. F.H.

Once again, W. H. Goss produced an accurate version of the Maldon device.

2. AIR RAID, WRECKAGE IN BAXTER AVENUE, SOUTHEND.

Above: This postcard was sent from Southend on 15 July 1915. The writer comments: 'Have you seen this card? Rather a narrow escape for mother.'

Right: Here is my rather fragile copy of the 'Air Raid Supplement', published by the *Southend Standard* on 13 May 1915. It is a remarkable document, full of eye-witness accounts. Note the ominous message dropped by the Zeppelin: 'You English. We have come and will come again. Kill or Cure. German.'

"SOUTHEND STANDARD"

Air Raid Supplement

THURSDAY, MAY 13, 1915.

1. Zeppelin Airship. 2. Message the Germans Left Behind. 3. Unexploded Bomb in Westborough Road Schools Playground.

BRITAIN'S CALL TO ZEPPELINS
"Zepp" this way!

Z N⁰ 100

NORTH SEA

We could certainly do without you
But we think you ought to come,
As old Kaiser Billy wants you
To taste a British gun!
He'd be sorry to lose you,
But with all his might and main,
He will cheer you! love you! kiss you!
IF you ever get back again!

I'd like to see the German who would
dare drop a bomb on me!

This isn't a Zeppelin Raid
in Southend-on-Sea
It's only the "Kid" having a
day at home

Above left: '"Zepp" this way!' is the invitation to the raider in a poetic verse.

Above right: This fearsome woman typifies the public's indignation and a determination to face whatever the Germans could muster.

Left: Versions of this card were overprinted with different towns.

Chapter Four: 'How Dare You Walk on our Front Door!'

The Kaiser had finally given his reluctant approval for the bombing of London east of a line parallel with the Tower of London and, on the night of 31 May/1 June, London was bombed for the first time by *LZ38*. The 20-minute raid from Stoke Newington to Stepney claimed seven lives and injured thirty-five.

This was a major propaganda coup, as the German public had clamoured for the Zeppelin to bring terror and panic to the streets and to strike at the enemy's heart. Postcard publishers were quick to oblige and the striking card at p. 37 parodies the pre-war 'Zeppelin Kommt' postcards also by the same artist, Arthur Thiele. His pre-war images depicted delighted citizens rushing to see the Zeppelin approaching their town. Now the tone was much darker.

Londoners were furious, and in Shoreditch mobs attacked and damaged a number of shops owned by persons believed to be of German nationality. Meanwhile, thousands paid a penny each to wander through the devastated houses where some of the victims had perished. This raid sparked the government into issuing D Notice 217 on 1 June, limiting coverage of the raids to official communications issued by the government.

Following the attack on London, and a major raid on Hull a few days later that killed twenty-six, simple air-raid precautions were introduced and the police issued instructions for the first time. However, it was up to local authorities to decide what to do. Warnings of raids were rudimentary and included policemen on foot or on bicycles with placards advising the public to 'Take Cover' or that it was 'All Clear'. Not until much later in the War was there any form of municipal shelter, and people were largely left to their own devices, being advised to take to cellars as the safest precaution.

Again, comic postcards showed the public's fortitude with the ubiquitous British umbrella being used as a defensive measure, or simply hiding under a lady's skirt. It was initially difficult to make people take shelter, as they would rush into the streets and stand gazing up at the intruder. There was also a fear, totally unfounded, that gas bombs would be dropped by Zeppelins, and almost at once gas masks of all kinds were on sale. Again, this additional danger found itself parodied in comic postcards.

Left: Sheltering in the cellar was one of the most common ways of keeping out of harm's way when the Zeppelin came to visit.

Below: On 17 May, *LZ38* bombed Ramsgate and a bomb struck the Bull and George Hotel.

VICTIMS OF AIR RAID
SOUTHEND-on-Sea
26, MAY, 1915.

Zeppelin kommt!

AIR RAID WARNING

"TAKING COVER"
IS ALL RIGHT.

Above left: A bomb fell on Mr Amstill's house at Southend on 26/27 May, killing his two little birds. Rather upset by their deaths, he sent this postcard to the Kaiser, but it was returned marked 'Not deliverable Enemy Country'.

Above right: Panicking Londoners take to the Underground station for safety, as the Zeppelin hovers over Tower Bridge. The back of this postcard includes a patriotic song of encouragement to terrorise London.

Right: An air raid warning from the police enables this little dog to enjoy 'taking cover'.

How to ENJOY the MOONLIGHT.
Get Insured and sit in the Cellar.

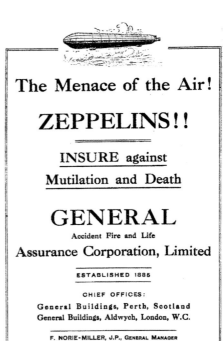

The Menace of the Air!

ZEPPELINS!!

INSURE against

Mutilation and Death

GENERAL

Accident Fire and Life

Assurance Corporation, Limited

ESTABLISHED 1885

CHIEF OFFICES:

General Buildings, Perth, Scotland
General Buildings, Aldwych, London, W.C.

F. NORIE-MILLER, J.P., GENERAL MANAGER

Assets as Security for Policy-holders
exceed — £2,500,000

WE 'RE PREPARED FOR
ZEPPELIN RAIDS !!

Above left: Deep in the cellar with insurance cover provided by the daily newspapers and *John Bull* magazine, these children and their dog are safe from a moonlight encounter with a Zeppelin.

Above right: Other cover was available, and this insurance company was not exactly subtle in its approach. A 10s premium for the duration of War, paid out up to £500, for your death or loss of limbs and/or sight.

Left: Children were often used on comic postcards to represent adult emotions.

I think I'm safe from Zepps here—they daren't spoil the boss's umbrella.

NOT TAKING ANY RISKS.

Above left: Hopefully, the boss's umbrella will keep this pup safe from bombardment.

Above right: If you were caught in the open during a raid, the advice was to lie down.

Right: Watching for the 'Zepps' was also a popular postcard theme.

"DEAR ME—HOW THE TIME DOES GO WHEN YOU'RE LOOKING FOR ZEPPELINS!"

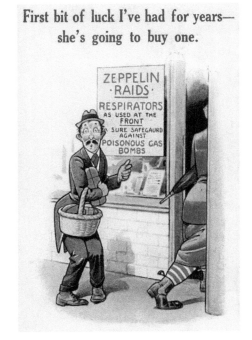

Above left: Will the Zeppelin commander see through Mr Brown's disguise?

Above right: Unfortunately for this henpecked husband, his wife didn't need to use a gas mask during the raids.

Below: What seems to be the whole of West Ham, assisted by the man in the moon, are up late to spot the raider.

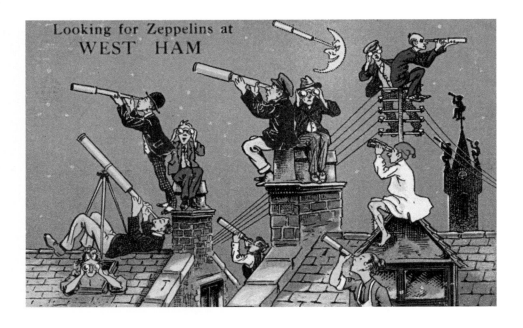

Chapter Five: The Forgotten Zeppelin 'Strafer' and a Trip to the East Coast

Three Army Zeppelins set out on a raid on 6/7 June 1915. One returned to its base in Belgium with engine trouble, and was bombed and destroyed in its shed. The others ran into thick fog and abandoned the raid. Flight Sub-Lieutenant Reginald 'Rex' Warneford, RNAS, flying a Morane-Sauliner Parasol, chased *LZ37* from the coast and succeeded in releasing six 20-lb bombs on the descending airship, the last of which caused it to explode. *LZ37* crashed into a large convent in Ghent, killing and injuring nuns and orphan children.

Warneford became an instant hero, an antidote to the frustration being felt at home due to the inability of the Home Defence to engage the raiders. He was promptly awarded the Victoria Cross. However, ten days later Warneford was killed when his plane crashed, carrying an American journalist, Henry Needham. The cause of the crash is a mystery: the aircraft, a Farman F27, turned over in the air and both men were thrown out. His passenger had been nervous about the flight, and one theory is that he panicked and grabbed the controls.

Due to his untimely death, Warneford is largely forgotten, his brave action being eclipsed by the exploits of Royal Flying Corps airmen in 1916.

Zeppelin raids continued throughout August and September, including Woodbridge in Suffolk and Dereham in Norfolk. These East Coast towns are largely unchanged today and, armed with contemporary postcards, you can easily find yourself transported back over 100 years, imagining the sights and sounds of the aftermath of a Zeppelin raid.

Guerre 1914-15... Le sous-lieutenant aviateur
Anglais WARNEFORD qui détruisit
un Zeppelin

War 1914-15.. English second-lieutenant
Aviator WARNEFORD who destroyed Visé, Paris N° 1200
a Zeppelin

A DUEL IN THE AIR.

Above left: Reginald 'Rex' Warneford, a talented RNAS pilot, was born in Darjeeling, India, in 1891. He was educated in England before returning to India, where he was apprenticed to the British India Steam Navigation Company.

Above right: Miraculously, one of *LZ37*'s crew survived, falling through an attic skylight and landing on a nun's (unoccupied) feather bed.

Below: St John's Hill, Woodbridge. The house at the right background with a tarpaulin on the roof is 27 New Road, where another person died.

Zeppelin Raid on Woodbridge August 12th. 1915.
The x indicates where Mr & Mrs. Tyler were killed. Publ. by: Stephenson Woodbridge.

Just outside Dereham, in a flagrant breach of health and safety rules, Barbara Gower and Margaret Kemp pose with a 110-lb unexploded high-explosive bomb, which was dropped nearby.

St John's Hill, Woodbridge – August 1915.

St John's Hill, Woodbridge. Photograph taken by the author in 2011.

Church Street, Dereham – September 1915.

Church Street, Dereham. Photograph taken by the author in 2015.

Above right and below: The public stayed positive despite the increasing number of raids; this card was sent in September 1915. Note the use of the anti-Zeppelin candlestick as a means of reducing light. Shelley produced a crested china version as a souvenir of the Great War.

Chapter Six: Help! Murder! The Zepps have Come!

The raid of 8/9 September on Central London was, in material terms, the most destructive of the entire war, with a 1915 valuation on the damage put at £530,787. Dubbed the 'Great Fire Raid', it was carried out by *Kapitanleutnant* Heinrich Mathy, the most daring and able of Germany's airship captains. Explosive and incendiary bombs fell across London from Golders Green to Liverpool Street station, causing severe damage. Fires engulfed the nearby garment manufacturing district. An eye-witness account is reproduced at p. 48, giving an indication of the intensity of the raid, which killed twenty-two and injured eighty-seven.

In the early days of the War, Special Constables received a good deal of ridicule, as their ad hoc uniform of civilian clothes and armlet was not an imposing representation of law enforcement. Specials assisted the regular police force in guarding vulnerable locations, such as pumping stations, and enforcing lighting orders. However, the bravery of this volunteer force was soon recognised, as they were on emergency call in the event of an air raid and faced falling bombs and shrapnel.

A few days after Mathy's raid, Sir Percy Scott, a retired admiral, was put in charge of London's defences. A gunnery expert, he scrambled together extra guns and was able to obtain of one of the latest French 75-mm auto-canons. The intense anti-aircraft fire from the improved London defences was in evidence during the raid on 13/14 October. This five-airship raid claimed seventy-one lives and was dubbed the 'Theatreland' raid, as *L15* dropped bombs along The Strand, Drury Lane and the Aldwych.

German propaganda postcards continued to proclaim that the raids on London were having a devastating effect, while British comic postcards continued to deflect the on-going Zeppelin threat. However, a fatalistic attitude was becoming more evident in the depictions of the trials and tribulations of life under bombardment.

Help! Murder!
The Zepps have come!

Right: The message on this card reads, 'This card put me in mind of the Saturday night when I was home.'

Below: The remains of the No. 8 bus, which suffered a direct hit just to the north of Liverpool Street. The driver and eight passengers were killed.

All that was left of a No. 8 'Bus after the Zeppelin raid on Wednesday, September 8, 1915.

SOUTH CROFTY LIMITED.

6. *Broad Street Place*
London E.C. 8th Septr. 1915.

Josiah Paull Esq

Dear Mr. Paull,

      You will no doubt be interested to know
that the Zepps. dropped a bomb just in front of our offices
last night, and have smashed nearly all our windows,
without, however, doing other material damage. Our
housekeeper informs me, however, that a bus was passing
at the time, and that five persons were killed. Certainly
there are ominous signs on the pavement. In our Board
Room the glass has been splintered, although ⅜" plate,
and pieces imbedded in the plaster across the room. The
bomb made a hole in the road about 6 feet across and 4 feet
deep, going through the wood paving and a foot of concrete.
The wood paving has been lifted for yards in all directions.
We have found in our Board Room pieces of wood and glass
from the bus, pieces of the wood pavement, and a small
piece of the bomb, which will no doubt be mounted and
suitably inscribed in due course. Personally, I had a

2.

splendid, though distant, view of the Zep. and the
shrapnel bursting round it. There is not the slightest
doubt it was damaged, though to what degree is not known
at present. The wildest rumours are, naturally, around,
including one that messages have been dropped stating that
they are returning tonight. Should the office be
further damaged I will advise you.

    Yours faithfully,

Above: This letter was written in the immediate aftermath of Mathy's raid and mentions the destruction of another bus, which was struck outside Broad Street station.

Below: London's full array of anti-aircraft guns failed to disrupt the Zeppelin from its course on the night of 8 September 1915.

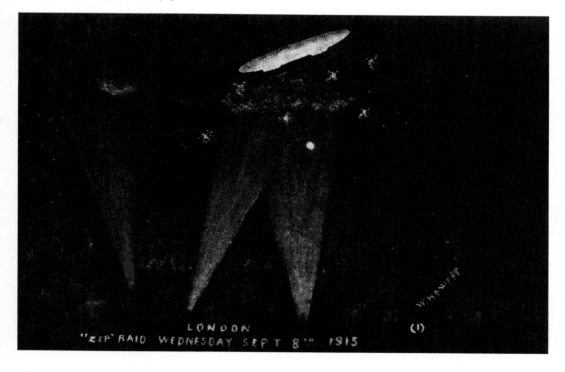

Right: Rather cheekily, Mathy (or more likely a member of his crew) dropped this ham bone attached to a parachute on Wrotham Park in Barnet as a memento from 'starved out' Germany.

Below left and right: This postcard is, perhaps, rather harsh on the volunteer special constables. However, here is a more affectionate take on the early days of the 'Specials' before proper uniforms were issued.

BONE WITH PARACHUTE DROPPED FROM A ZEPPELIN IN WROTHAM PARK, BARNET. 8TH SEPTEMBER 1915.

EDWARD GREY . POOR DEVIL! WHAT AM I TO DO?

IN REMEMBRANCE OF STARVED OUT GERMANY.

UNDER A SPREADING CHESNUT TREE
THESE SPECIALS NIGHTLY STAND,
EACH WITH A BOTTLE AS YOU SEE,
A RED-NOSED HAPPY BAND. COPYRIGHT

Our Special Constable.

By George - a beastly bomb - what!

Waiting for
BOMBS

at TUNBRIDGE WELLS

GUERRE AERILNNE — L'Auto-Canon
qui détruisit le Zeppelin le 21 Février 1916
AERIAL WAR - The Auto-Canon which
destroyed the Zeppelin on the 21ª Feb 1916

Above left: Boy scouts were pressed into service. Their duties included sounding bugles to give the all clear after a raid and assisting the military, hospitals and other organisations – but not bomb disposal.

Above right: An example of the auto-canon that Sir Percy Scott was able to obtain. It had already proved successful against the Zeppelin on the Western Front.

Below: Zeppelins over Trafalgar Square spreading panic in this German propaganda postcard sent on 30 October 1915. Just three weeks earlier, *L15* had crossed this iconic landmark as it commenced its bombing run.

1.Drv.C.J.Tarrant.
2.Drv.F. Kreppell.
3.Cond'r.E.G.Harvey.
4.Cond'r.C. Rogers.

These men met an untimely end, the result of Zeppelin raids.

Das Schwert des Damokles.

Above left: The faces of the bus drivers and conductors who perished in the September and October 1915 raids. Some 150 white-coated drivers paraded behind the funeral cortege of Driver Tarrant and Conductor Rogers on 20 October, and thousands lined the route.

Above right: The Sword of Damocles hovers over a cowering John Bull in the Tower of London.

Below: The 'Stormbird' dominates the London skyline. From the sale of each copy of this postcard, 2 pfennigs were donated to the German Red Cross.

Heil Zeppelins Sturmvögel!

LOOKING FOR ZEPPELINS.
THOSE WHO LOOK OUT OF THE WINDOW
DON'T SEE MOST OF THE "BOMBS."

Poor soul! I wonder if she's been hit with a Zeppelin Bomb.

These raiders make you feel very unsettled—if they dropped a bomb here they'd blow this screen to smithereens!

Above left: In contrast to the German postcard publishers' take on the Zeppelin raids, the British attitude to events remained full of humour. This young gentleman looks for a different sort of 'bomb', or 'bombshell'.

Above right: Even the prospect of a grizzly death by Zeppelin bomb was put sharply into comic relief. The message on this card reads: 'No the Zepps didn't pay a visit here this time'.

Left: The young lady behind the screen is a little anxious about a raid interrupting her ablutions.

"Who said Zepps"

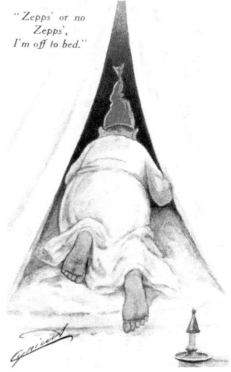

"Zepps' or no
Zepps',
I'm off to bed."

Above left: With the protection of an umbrella, a makeshift gas mask and a cash box tucked under her arm, this little girl is taking every precaution in the event of a raid.

Above right: This character in his nightgown lives up to the name of the artist, Cynicus, who designed this card.

Right: A despairing builder bemoans the additional work that the increasing number of Zeppelin raids has caused.

"THIS WILL BE THE THIRD TIME I'VE PUT
THAT BLOOMING ROOF ON!"
"Ça va faire la troisième fois que je répare ce toit!"

Chapter Seven: 'A Zep in the Right Direction'

The Zeppelins returned in force on 31 January 1916; there was a nine-airship raid on the Midlands, which was less well defended than London. The raid left seventy dead and over 100 injured. One of the night's raiders was *L19*, which experienced engine and wireless failure on its return journey.

The next morning, the floating wreck of the airship was discovered by a British steam fishing trawler, the *King Stephen*, commanded by William Martin. Clinging to the wreck was the sixteen-man crew. Martin refused to rescue them and sailed away, leaving the crew to its fate. The resulting furore was seized on by German postcard publishers for propaganda purposes.

On 31 March 1916, *L22* attacked Cleethorpes in Lincolnshire, where a bomb scored a direct hit on a Baptist chapel, which had just become the billet of B Company, 3rd Battalion of the Manchester Regiment. The bomb killed twenty-seven soldiers instantly and, of the fifty-three injured, another five died later.

The night also marked the loss of *L15*. It was hit by the Woolwich anti-aircraft gun and received a direct hit from the gun at Purfleet, Essex. As the damaged airship descended, it was also attacked by Second Lieutenant Alfred de Bathe Brandon, armed with a combination of incendiary bombs and explosive darts.

Eventually, the Zeppelin became too heavy to fly and came down in the sea off Margate at 12.15 a.m. on 1 April. The half-sunk remains were then taken under tow, but the airship broke up off Westgate and only small sections were hauled ashore.

A ZEP IN THE RIGHT DIRECTION.

MRS. ALICE EDWARDS, Age 28, November 9th, who lost her Leg in the Air Raid in the Midlands, on January 31st, 1916, and had the Raid Baby born on June 18th.

Above left: 1916 marked a change in the fortunes of the defending forces.

Above right: The front of a house in Union Street, Tipton, was blown in, killing Arthur Edwards. His pregnant wife, Alice, shown here with her 'Raid Baby', lost a leg.

Below: 'Faithful to the End'. The loss of *L19* received worldwide publicity and divided public opinion.

GUERRE AÉRIENNE   Chute du
Zeppelin L. 19 dans la Mer du Nord

AERIAL WAR — The Fall of the
Zeppelin L. 19. in the North sea   Visé, Paris

Above: An artist's impression of the *King Stephen* incident. She never sailed as a fishing vessel again and was taken over by the Royal Navy for use as a Q-ship, before being sunk twelve weeks later.

Below left: This memorial at Cleethorpes Cemetery to the worst single incident in all of the Zeppelin raids was raised by public subscription.

Below right: Another cause of a 'Zeppelin Night'.

THE ZEPPELIN SINKING IN THE THAMES ESTUARY, SATURDAY, APRIL 1ST 1916.
— DAILY SKETCH PHOTOGRAPH.

Above: One crew member of *L15* was drowned, and the rest were rescued by the armed trawler *Olivine* and then transferred to the destroyer, HMS *Vulture*. *Vulture*'s captain demanded that the Zeppelin's crew strip and board in groups of three.

Right: Alfred de Bathe Brandon was born in Wellington, New Zealand, in 1883 and studied law at Trinity College, Cambridge, before returning home to join his father's legal practice. On the outbreak of the war he returned to England to qualify as a pilot.

COPYRIGHT.
SPORT & GENERAL.   LIEUT. A. BRANDON, D.S.O., M.C.   BEAGLES POSTCARDS.
THE GALLANT AIRMAN WHO GAINED HIS DECORATION
FOR SUCCESSFULLY ATTACKING ENEMY AIRSHIPS.

Come away, my dears—perhaps it's a wrecked Zeppelin.

Above and Below left: Publisher Bamforth was also quick to recognise the demise of *L19* and *L15*. These cards were sent on 16 May and 27 July 1916 respectively.

Below right: A satirical 'In Memoriam' postcard to the *L15*, with suitable prose.

Oh! Anuver recked Zeppelum in the Norf Sea!

In Never
Loving Memory
OF L-15.

Laid to Rest in the Thames Estuary, April Fool's Day, 1916.

Here lie the remains of a raiding Zep,
Which from Germany came while our children
slept,
Our Terriers gallantly manned their guns,
And brought down the cultured murdering
Huns,
To whom we can say should we near them be,
"Go to *L-15*—at the bottom of the sea."

Above: Pieces of the recovered wreckage of *L15* were fashioned into crude souvenirs and widely circulated.

Right: Poetic praise for the gunners and searchlight crews, now better organised and equipped to combat the Zeppelin menace. Each officer and man on duty with London's anti-aircraft units on the night of 31 March/1 April received a gold medal courtesy of the Lord Mayor of London. Sir Charles Wakefield had offered a bounty of £500 to the first gun crew to shoot down a Zeppelin on domestic soil. Due to the fact that a number of gun crews were involved in shooting down *L15*, it was decided that the money would instead be spent on the production of the medals.

HERE'S TO THE GUNNERS.

PRAISE God, from whom all blessings flow,
    And thank the gunners too ;
And the men who worked the searchlights,
    So the Zepp dared not come through.
They saved us from some loss of life,
    They saved us loss of wealth :
Hear's to the gunners and their mates ;
    To them long life and health.

The villain had it in for us,
    Of bombs, on board he'd tons,
And we'd have suffered frightf'ly, had
    It not been for the guns.
He thought to catch us napping,
    But the searchlights stopped his stealth,
Here's to the gunners and their mates,
    To them long life and health.

Cartledge, Publisher.

Chapter Eight: 'Zepparation Allowance'

On 2/3 September 1916, the Germans mounted their largest raid of the war, with sixteen airships taking part. The task force was scattered by storms over the North Sea, but an Army Schütte-Lanz type, *SL11*, pressed on to London. Enter the man who inspired this book: Lieutenant William Leefe Robinson of 39 Squadron, Royal Flying Corps.

Robinson had taken off in his converted BE2c biplane from Suttons Farm airfield at Hornchurch at 11.08 p.m. and, after almost three hours in the air, he was nearing the end of his patrol. However, he noticed a red glow to the north-east of London, where bombs had been dropped by *SL11* and went to investigate.

At 2.14 a.m., the Waltham Abbey searchlights and gun locked on to the airship and Robinson raced towards it. After closing in and firing three drums of the recently introduced incendiary ammunition upwards into *SL11*, it caught fire and, in full view of the Metropolis, fell in a roaring mass of flame, striking the ground at Cuffley.

Millions of Londoners cheered the unknown hero who had been the first to shoot down an airship over mainland Britain. The fall of the airship, described as 'a stupendous blazing torch plunging down with incredible swiftness', was rapidly reproduced on a wide range of postcards.

Railway whistles blew and factory hooters were sounded, while people poured on into the streets, singing and dancing. It was a wonderful tonic, coming shortly after the indecisive naval battle at Jutland and in light of the lengthy casualty lists from the Somme.

On Sunday 3 September, which was later referred to as 'Zepp Sunday', news of Robinson's victory spread with incredible speed. This airship was deliberately described officially and in the press as 'Zeppelin L21' for propaganda purposes, and this misidentification persisted for decades.

Over the next two days, over 10,000 people travelled to the tiny village, and police and troops were called in to control the crowds. There was a scramble for souvenirs, although keeping pieces of airship was a punishable offence.

A Victoria Cross winner, Robinson became a reluctant national hero, feted wherever he went, and received significant amounts of prize money and other gifts. Soon, even the smallest pieces of wire and debris from the downed airship were being kept as keepsakes or sold for war charities.

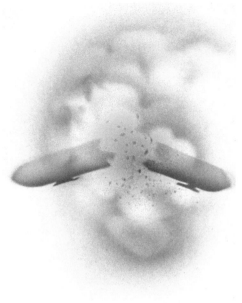

ZEPPARATION ALLOWANCE

THE 'ROBINSON' TOUCH
an impression by an eyewitness - 20 miles away.

Airship brought down in flames at Cuffley, Herts, by
FLIGHT-LIEUT. W. L. ROBINSON, V.C., Sept. 3rd, 1916.
Sanctioned by Censor, Press Bureau, Sept. 22nd, 1916.

Above left: Armed with incendiary ammunition, the tide was turned.

Above right: An artist's impression of the outcome of the aerial duel above London. *SL11* had a length of 570 feet and a diameter of 66 feet, whilst Robinson's BE2c had a length of just 27 feet and a wingspan of 37 feet.

Right: William Leefe Robinson was the youngest of seven children, born at Pollibetta, South Coorg, in Southern India in 1895. He was wounded as an RFC observer on the Western Front in 1915, before qualifying as a pilot.

A SOUVENIR
*of the destruction of Zeppelin L.16 by
Lieut. W. L. Robinson V.C. at Cuffley*

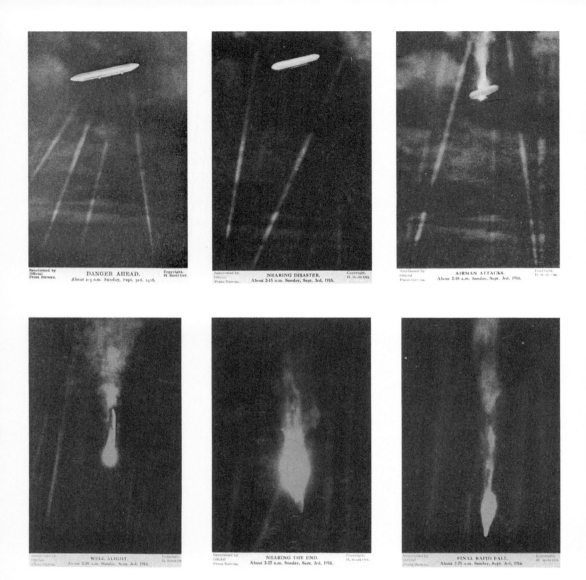

A series of postcards chronicling the demise of *SL11*. Londoners were awoken by a crescendo of noise and tumbled from their beds to watch the spectacle that unfolded in the skies above them.

Coming down!

Above left: Biscuit manufacturer Walker Harrison & Garthwaites published this card as part of its 'VC Winners' series.

Above right and Below right: Artist G. E. Shepheard depicted the fall of the airship in the form of the Kaiser with his famous moustache burning and the hapless crew landing in a heap.

The Hun-expected invasion of England.

Here is a more macabre representation of the event. The entire crew of *SL11* perished, including its English-born commander, Wilhelm Schramm. They were buried at Mutton Lane Cemetery, in nearby Potters Bar, with military honours.

Lieut. William Leefe Robinson, V.C.

Within days, Robinson had received the Victoria Cross from the King at Windsor. His image was everywhere, and Cuffley became world famous as the news spread across the globe.

ROMFORD SOUVENIR OF THE HERO WHO BROUGHT DOWN ZEP. "L.21" AT CUFFLEY ON SEP. 3RD 1916.

LIEU. WILLIAM LEEFE ROBINSON, V.C.

Another souvenir postcard, with the hero encircled by the RFC wings. Romford is close to Suttons Farm airfield.

3787 F   ROTARY PHOTO. F.C.
"STRAFED" BY LIEUT. WILLIAM LEEFE ROBINSON V.C.
CUFFLEY, 3RD SEPT. 1916.

Right: 'The man behind the Gun'.

Below: The crash site at Cuffley with one of *SL11*'s Maybach engines visible. Note the swathes of wire and small pieces of debris.

3787 B   THE WRECKED ZEPPELIN, CUFFLEY, 3RD SEPT., 1916.   ROTARY PHOTO. E.C.

THE ZEPPELIN'S DIVE TO DEATH
SUNDAY SEPT 3rd 1916.

E & H. SCOONES   WALBROOK. E.C.

Above left and right: The burning airship lit up the ground below for a radius of over 60 miles. German Army airships never raided Britain again. The reverse of the postcard describes the fall of *L32*, which was destroyed in similar circumstances.

Left: Robinson received £4,200 in prize money, some of which was used to buy this new 'Prince Henry' Vauxhall car.

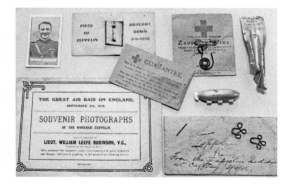

A selection of Robinson and *SL11* mementoes. By November 1916, over £3,000 had been raised by the sale of Red Cross Zeppelin relics in London alone.

Chapter Nine: 'Our Anti-Zeptic Treatment is quite a Success'

After Robinson's success, the Home Defence squadrons were inspired. A raid on 23 September 1916, including three of the new 'super' Zeppelins, headed for the capital. To the east of London, *L33* was caught in the searchlights and riddled by the ground guns. With a gas cell ruptured, it began to fly an erratic course and was also attacked by Lieutenant Brandon of *L15* fame. The crew started to throw any removable objects overboard to keep the airship aloft, but to no avail.

An hour later, *L33* crash-landed in a field between Little Wigborough and Peldon in Essex. There was so little gas left in the airship that only the outer casing would burn and it was recovered virtually intact. The commander, Alois Böcker, gathered his crew together and they set off towards Peldon. Travelling on his bicycle in the opposite direction, attracted by the fire, was Special Constable Edgar Nicholas, who was surprised by the sudden appearance of a body of men marching along a lane in the early hours of the morning. Escorting the Germans to the local post office, Police Constable Charles Smith took charge and formally arrested the crew.

L32 was also picked up by searchlights and Second Lieutenant Frederick Sowrey, Robinson's close friend from 39 Squadron, attacked. Again, incendiary ammunition sent the raider down in flames. The wreckage, which lay at Snails Farm, Great Burstead, near Billericay, Essex, drew huge crowds the following morning, as did the skeleton of *L33*. Both wrecks were put under guard and there was, once again, an insatiable desire for souvenirs from the crowds who descended on the latest crash sites. Farmhands, soldiers, policemen and fire officers made an easy profit selling scraps of metal and fabric to the unending stream of visitors.

Our
Anti-Zeptic
Treatment
is quite a
Success.

Taking Robinson's lead, further successes soon followed.

The publication of this photograph is permitted by the Official Press Bureau, on condition that this card is not sent out of the country or put on sale. The Managing Director has also a printed page from the log of the Zeppelin showing the places at which it should call, but publication of this is not permitted.

Machine Gun dropped on Tiptree Hall Farm from the Zeppelin brought down in the neighbourhood on September 24th, 1916. Photographed by Mr. S. S. WILKIN.

This advertising card was issued by Wilkin & Sons, makers of Tiptree Jam. The factory was on the route of *L33*'s unsuccessful escape attempt.

WRECKAGE   CROWN COPYRIGHT RES.

A side view of the wreckage of *L33*, which dwarfs nearby New Hall Cottages.

An artist's impression of the capture of *L33*'s crew. The English-speaking commander calmly asked the Special Constable, 'How many miles is it to Colchester?'

THE CREW OF ZEPPELIN L33, TWENTY-TWO IN NUMBER, BROUGHT DOWN ON THE ESSEX COAST DURING THE EARLY HOURS OF SUNDAY, SEPT. 24TH, 1916. A SPECIAL CONSTABLE APPEARED ON THE SCENE, AND IN THE WORDS OF A LOCAL RUSTIC—"HE TOOK UP THE WHOLE OF 'EM."

The Peldon 'Specials' outside the Peldon Plough. Special Constable Edgar Nicholas is standing on the left.

The Eight Essex Special Constables who arrested Zeppelin Crew, September 24th. 1916.

Hallo ! Another Zepp down.

Comic postcards continued to revel in the demise of the Zeppelin.

Above: The tangled mass of wreckage of *L32*. Note the sheer quantity of the duralumin framework in contrast to the scant remains of the wooden-framed *SL11* at Cuffley.

Left: A portrait of Frederick Sowrey, who was born in Gloucestershire in 1893. An infantry officer, he was wounded at the Battle of Loos before transferring to the RFC. He had a distinguished RAF career, retiring as a group captain in May 1940.

LIEUT. SOWREY, D.S.O.
Photo—Topical.

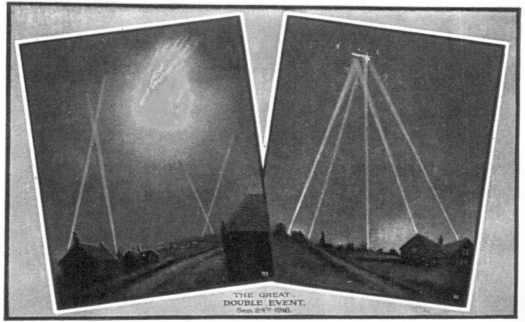

THE GREAT
DOUBLE EVENT.
Sep. 24ᵗʰ 1916.

Sanctioned by Censor, Press Bureau, September 30th, 1916.

The 'Great Double Event' was a major turning point, with the loss of two of the newest Zeppelins and their most experienced pilots.

PORT.SIDE.ELEVATOR.L33.SOMEWHERE.IN.ESSEX.

Part of *L33* being removed for analysis. The remains were of great value in their almost completely preserved state, which enabled the designers of the British airship programme to adapt their plans and produce near copy designs.

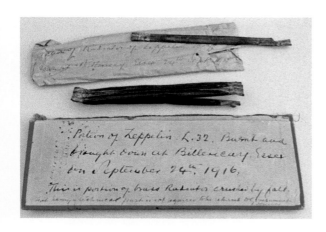

Portion of Zeppelin L.32 Burnt and brought down at Billericay Essex on September 24th 1916. This is portion of brass Radiator crushed by fall...

79½ Pauli avenue, Cricklewood
4th Oct: 1916

My dear Dick

I send you as a memento of no doubt the saddest time in your life when you lost one of the bravest and best of sons.

This piece of the Zeppelin L.32 was given me by a naval aircraft man who was on the scene of its downfall. The brass tubes were cylindrical but the heat of the burning and the fall of 3 or 4 miles downwards flattened them out. If you do not care to keep it then give it to some Museum in memory of your brave son — Jo sent me a copy of the Irish Times with the age of his death. It shews how you all were respected.

I hope now you and Maggie are feeling more resigned to the great Creators will. God bless you all. Yours very sincere

T. Arthur.

Souvenirs of *L32*, the first highly personal and the second a mass-produced item.

Since the Zeppelins have come to Town
  I always wear my best night gown,
And tie my hair with a big blue bow
  In case they call on me you know.

" Zeppelins again !
—and my hair in Curlpapers."

A pair of charming postcards. The second card was sent on 27 September 1916 from Haringey, North London, with the message: 'You will see by this card that the girls here are more vain than patriotic. Glad you are not troubled with gasbags.'

Damage by Air Raids in the East End.
A Bedroom in the "Black Swan" Public House,
after the Zepp Raid.

L33 had successfully dropped bombs to the east of London, including the destruction of a public house on Bow Road, before its demise.

Comic postcard publishers often featured pubs, which were a focal point of communities despite the restrictions to licencing hours.

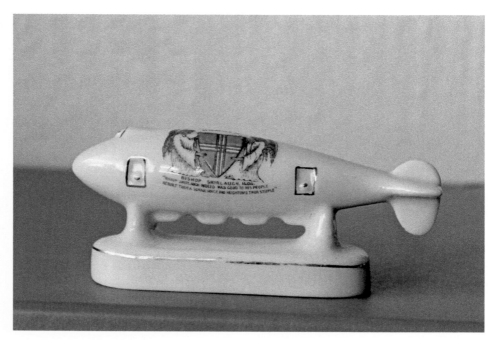

Savoy China registered a totally inaccurate design for the 'super' Zeppelin just four days after the Double Event.

Chapter Ten: 'Because I Love the Flying Man Who Bombs the Zeppelin'

On board *L31*, on the night of 1 October 1916, Heinrich Mathy led a formation of eleven Zeppelins. It was his fifteenth raid over England. Approaching London from the north, the guns below responded and Mathy had to turn away, but, unfortunately for him, Second Lieutenant Wulstan Tempest, another 39 Squadron pilot, had struggled up to around 15,000 feet while stalking the airship. Tempest attacked resolutely, in the face of heavy machine-gun fire, and *L31* went down in flames, piling up on the outskirts of Potters Bar. As at Cuffley and in Essex, sightseers and souvenir hunters thronged to the crash site.

Following Robinson's success, the Hornchurch Parish Council asked for subscriptions to present him with a silver cup. Over 3,000 donations were received and, when Sowrey and Tempest repeated the feat, it was decided to include them as well and each pilot received a handsome trophy.

Promoted to Captain, William Leefe Robinson survived the war, but not much longer. He was shot down and taken prisoner on 5 April 1917 while flying a Bristol F.2A on the Western Front. Robinson had a harsh time in captivity, largely due to the notoriety attached to his VC. Nevertheless, he made a number of escape attempts. His health suffered while a prisoner and he fell sick with influenza when being repatriated after the Armistice. He died on 31 December 1918 and is buried at Harrow Weald.

Following further losses in November 1916, there would not be any more serious attacks for several months while the Germans licked their wounds. Subsequently, during 1917, the air raid initiative passed from airships to aeroplanes, in the form of the twin-engine Gotha bomber and the Giant Zeppelin-Staaken R-plane.

NEITHER JACK NOR TOMMY CAN
MY WHOLE AFFECTIONS WIN,
BECAUSE I LOVE THE FLYING MAN
WHO BOMBS THE ZEPPELIN.

LIEUT. W. J. TEMPEST. D.S.O.
THIS DISTINGUISHED AIRMAN GAINED HIS DECORATION FOR CONSPICUOUS
GALLANTRY AND DEVOTION TO DUTY
IN CONNECTION WITH THE DESTRUCTION OF AN ENEMY AIRSHIP.

Above left: All the nice girls love an airman. Robinson and his fellow 'Zepp Slayers' were pursued by female admirers, and their airfield came under virtual siege.

Above right: Wulstan Tempest was born in Yorkshire in 1891. Like Sowrey, he was wounded in action (Ypres 1914) before transferring to the RFC. He added the Military Cross to his DSO for his work in command of a night-bombing squadron and retired from the RAF, retaining the rank of major.

The Barnet Searchlight Detachment was commended for its assistance in holding *L31* in the beams of the Tramway searchlight and aiding Tempest's attack.

Right: Celebrating the fourth setback for the raiders in under a month.

Below: The main portion of *L31* wrapped itself around an oak tree. The 'Zeppelin Oak' became a local monument until it was cut down in the 1930s. Note the crowds behind the fences erected by the Army.

"THE FOURTH"!!!!
Super-Zeppelin brought down in Flames at Potters Bar, Oct. 1st, 1916.
Reproduced by premission of "THE DAILY SKETCH."

Again, parts of the wreckage were fashioned into souvenirs. This piece was presented to an RFC officer.

The Man who says "I saw it all from start to finish !"

Celui qui dit qu'il a vu descendre le Zeppelin.

ZEPPS!

While Zeppelins no longer attempted to attack London, the German Naval Airship Division turned its attention to the industrial areas in the north. However, the public still had to deal with inconvenience of life under aerial bombardment.

THREE GALLANT AIRMEN. - "THE ZEPPELIN STRAFERS."

LIEUT. ROBINSON, V.C   LIEUT. TEMPEST, D.S.O.   LIEUT. SOWREY, D.S.O.

The three gallant 'Zeppelin Strafers' were widely featured on postcards and in magazines.

If airmen are flying about this night
    I hope they'll see a smile that charms,
For I'm wishing and wishing with all my
        might,
    That one will fly into my arms!

"I say you two, come out of that cellar. The Airship's been gone ever so long!"

As one lady wishes for a visit from a brave airman like Robinson and his pals, it was time for couples to finally come out from the safety of their cellars.

79

As befitted their celebrity status, the autographs of Robinson and Sowrey were highly prized by the public. 'Robin' was one of Robinson's nicknames.

Presentation of cups to the three Zeppelin heroes, by residents of an Essex village. Captain L. W. Robinson, V.C., receiving his cup.

The presentation of three Zeppelin Cups took place at the New Zealand Soldiers' Convalescent Hospital Camp at Grey Towers Mansion, Hornchurch, on 14 October 1916. By coincidence, this was where 'Rex' Warneford had his first taste of military life in the Sportsman's Battalion in January 1915.

Feldwebel Sebastian Festner of *Jasta* 11 was credited with the victory over Robinson's Bristol fighter. The Jasta (squadron) was commanded by Manfred von Richthofen. Festner was killed in action just twenty days later.

On the evening of 27 November 1916, eight Zeppelins reached the British coast. *L34* was destroyed near West Hartlepool by Second Lieutenant Ian Pyott of 36 Squadron. The Zeppelin was captained by Max Dietrich, an uncle of the singer and actress Marlene Dietrich.

The end of a Zeppelin in the North Sea Nov. 28. 1916. (passed for publication by the press Bureau Nov. 29.16)

Further south, near Lowestoft, *L21* suffered a similar fate at the hands of RNAS pilots, one of whom, Flight Sub-Lieutenant Edward Pulling, is pictured with his BE2c.

Above: A six-inch piece of *L34*, retrieved from the North Sea.

Left: The men of the Barnet Searchlight Station certainly had a Merry Christmas.

Chapter Eleven: 'I Thought I Saw a Zepp Here Today'

In March 1917, the first raid by the latest class of Zeppelin, known as the 'height-climbers', took place. These airships had a much higher operational ceiling and the ability to climb up to 21,000 feet, well beyond the range of anti-aircraft guns and fighter aircraft.

On 17 June, the 644-foot-long *L48*, a 'high-climber' on its first mission over England, encountered engine problems and a frozen compass. It was soon engaged by the guns and attacked by three separate aircraft. It broke into a huge 'V' and fell in flames into a field at Holly Tree farm near Theberton, Suffolk. There were three survivors out of nineteen crew members: the first and last Zeppelin crew members to survive the crash of a burning airship over England. One subsequently died of his injuries.

On 19/20 October 1917, the last major Zeppelin raid took place, with eleven airships ordered to attach the industrial region of 'middle England'. Known as the 'silent raid' due to the height at which the Zeppelins flew, it was a disaster. The efficiency of the crews was impaired by altitude sickness and intense cold, and a strong gale swept the Zeppelins blindly south. London was bombed for the final time by *L45*, as the airship sped past the capital. Four Zeppelins were lost that night.

The last act of the Zeppelin as a raider occurred on 5 August 1918, when five Zeppelins flew up the coast of Norfolk. No bombs were dropped on any land target, but *L70*, the latest in airship construction, was attacked by aircraft and erupted in flames. On board was Peter Strasser, the inspirational and charismatic *'Führer der Luftschiffe'*. To the end, he maintained an unshaken belief in the value of the Zeppelin as a weapon of war, despite mounting losses.

I THOUGHT I SAW A ZEPP
HERE TO-DAY

J'ai eu peur! . . je croyais que c'était un Zeppelin!

Zeppelin raids became less frequent in 1917 but the threat remained in the public's consciousness.

On 7 March 1917, Count von Zeppelin died aged seventy-nine. On his left is Dr Hugo Eckener, who was responsible for training airship pilots and went on to command the Graf Zeppelin. On the right is *'Führer der Luftschiffe'* (Leader of Airships) Peter Strasser. He was a hands-on commander, often accompanying his crews on their missions over England.

THE STRAFED ZEPP. 17th June, 1917. No. 4. Published by J. S. Waddell, Photographer, Leiston

A local photographer, J. S. Waddell of Leiston, issued a seventeen-postcard set showing the crash site and wreckage of *L48*, together with a number of other postcards and a commemorative booklet.

84

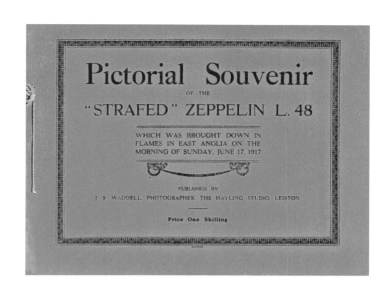

Again, the wreckage was used to create a range of keepsakes.

The remains of one of *L48*'s three engine gondolas.

By gum! it gave me a start—
I thought it was a Zeppelin.

WHO BROKE THAT PLATE, MARY?
I DON'T KNOW MUM. IT MUST HAVE BEEN ONE OF THEY ZEPPERLINS!

Present or not, 'Zepperlins' still got the blame for any minor accidents or scares.

German Graves, Theberton.

The graves of the crew members at St Peter's Church, Theberton. In the early 1960s, the remains were exhumed and re-buried at the German war cemetery at Cannock Chase, Staffordshire, along with the crews of *SL11*, *L31* and *L32*.

A triumphant postcard rejoicing in the mounting airship losses, possibly inspired by the 1917 music hall song 'Ten Little Zeppelins'.

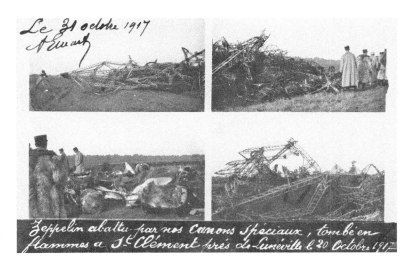

TEN STRAFING ZEPPELINS DROPPING BOMBS SO FINE UP CAME ROBINSON THEN THERE WERE NINE.	**10 STRAFING ZEPPELINS**	FIVE STRAFING ZEPPELINS HOVERED O'ER THE SHORE MASKED BATTERY OPEN'D FIRE THEN THERE WERE FOUR.

TEN STRAFING ZEPPELINS
DROPPING BOMBS SO FINE
UP CAME ROBINSON
THEN THERE WERE NINE.

NINE STRAFING ZEPPELINS
STAYED OUT TOO LATE
ONE MET SOWERY
THEN THERE WERE EIGHT.

EIGHT STRAFING ZEPPELINS
SAILED TOWARDS HEAVEN
BRANDON BARRED THE WAY
THEN THERE WERE SEVEN.

SEVEN STRAFING ZEPPELINS
IN AN AWFUL FIX
CAME ACROSS TEMPEST
THEN THERE WERE SIX.

SIX STRAFING ZEPPELINS
ESCAPE COULDN'T CONTRIVE
ONE STOPPED SOME SHRAPNEL
THEN THERE WERE FIVE.

FIVE STRAFING ZEPPELINS
HOVERED O'ER THE SHORE
MASKED BATTERY OPEN'D FIRE
THEN THERE WERE FOUR.

FOUR STRAFING ZEPPELINS
HOOKED IT TO SEA
DESTROYER MADE GOOD HIT
THEN THERE WERE THREE.

THREE STRAFING ZEPPELINS
'GAINST SKY SO BLUE
ONE HAD A MISHAP
THEN THERE WERE TWO.

TWO STRAFING ZEPPELINS
TRIED TO DODGE A GUN
TOMMY MADE GOOD SHOT
THEN THERE WAS ONE.

ONE STRAFING ZEPPELIN
COULDN'T SEE THE FUN
SO CAME DOWN TO EARTH
THEN THERE WAS NONE.

ONE POOR COUNT ZEPPELIN, IN AN AWFUL RAGE,
"WHERE ARE MY AIRSHIPS?" SEARCH *OUR* HISTORY'S PAGE! G.L.H.

One of the stricken Zeppelins of the 'Silent Raid', *L44* was shot down over France.

L64 was involved in some of the final ineffective raids during 1918 and was handed over to the British as part of the German reparations at the end of the War.

Chapter Twelve: 'I Hear There's Been a Raid up Your Way'

By early 1917, aviation technology had advanced to such an extent that biplanes with a bomb load of 1,000 lbs could now successfully reach England from bases in occupied Belgium.

Seventeen Gotha bombers struck London in the first daylight raid on the capital on 13 June 1917, causing 162 deaths and over 400 injuries. A few weeks later, the second and final daylight raid on London took place, causing further death and destruction.

Subsequent raids took place at night and the Gothas were joined by the massive Staaken 'Giant' R-plane. Well-armed and flying in formation, the Gotha presented a formidable challenge to the defending forces, which were in the process of being scaled back. To meet this latest threat, new tactics in aerial combat were developed and, by May 1918, over sixty Gothas had been destroyed; the threat to Britain was effectively at an end. The raids caused a similar amount of material damage as the airship raids. However, casualty figures were higher, with 837 people killed and a little under 2,000 injured.

In contrast to the wide range of comic postcards available that deal with the Zeppelin menace, references to raiding Gothas are scarcer to find. At best, postcard publishers recycled existing themes and images. The physical and psychological impact of the Gotha raids was far greater than those carried out by Zeppelins. This was particularly evident in the response to those attacks made in broad daylight, which lead to rioting taking place once again in London. Coastal towns in Essex and Kent were also attacked, often as an alternative target. Due to this increased anti-German feeling, George V decided to change the name of his royal house from Saxe-Coburg-Gotha to Windsor.

With a war-weary nation now subject to rationing and increased press censorship, the lack of postcards and souvenirs is not unsurprising. Even the few German postcards of this final phase of the air war on Britain are sombre in comparison to the strident imagery at the start of the conflict.

Hauptmann Brandenburg

Above left: The raiders came in all shapes and sizes.

Above right: In March 1917, Hauptmann Ernst Brandenburg was appointed commander of the *Englandgeschwader* ('the English Squadron') to carry out a daylight bombing offensive.

A Gotha G.V being loaded with bombs. Note the full night-bomber camouflage.

A swarm of black specks moving across the summer sky. The Home Defence forces were unprepared for the switch to daylight raids.

Portion of WINGED BOMB dropped by GERMAN AEROPLANE on Wednesday, 13th June, 1917, at 11.40 a.m. After exploding in mid air it fell in the vicinity of the Works.
Length - 19½ inches.   Diameter - 7 inches   Weight - 4 lbs.

A rare image of part of a Gotha's deadly payload.

Damage by Day-Light Air Raid in the East End.
North Street School — Ground Floor.
Searching the Debris.

Among the dead of the Gotha raid of 13 June 1917 were sixteen children, killed when a bomb fell on a primary school in Poplar.

A variation on the 'looking for Zeppelins' theme.

An unusual 'ruin'd rime' postcard, probably describing the Gotha raids of September and October 1917.

Hark I hear a Gotha !

Hark ! I hear a Zeppelin !

One of the few examples of the reuse of an earlier comic card to refer to the advent of the Gotha.

"Come on Billy We're safe here."

Another recycled image – see p. 8.

Der Deutsche Michel (the German equivalent of John Bull) cradles a Gotha on its journey to London.

Select Bibliography

Castle, H.G., *Fire Over England, The German Raids of World War I* (London: Leo Cooper in association with Secker & Warburg, 1982)

Castle, Ian, *The First Blitz – Bombing London in the First World War* (Oxford: Osprey Publishing, 2015)

Castle, Ian, *The Zeppelin Base Raids Germany 1914* (Oxford: Osprey Publishing, 2011)

De Syon, Guillaume, *Zeppelin! Germany and the Airship, 1900-1939* (Baltimore: The John Hopkins University Press, 2002)

Fegan, Thomas, *The 'Baby Killers' – German Air Raids on Britain in the First World War* (Barnsley: Leo Cooper, 2002)

Gibson, Mary, *Warneford, VC* (Yeovilton: The Fleet Air Arm Museum, 1979)

Hanson, Neil, *First Blitz* (London: Corgi Books, 2009)

Holt, Tonnie and Valmai, *Till the Boys Come Home: The Picture Postcards of the First World War* (London: Macdonald and Jane's, 1977)

Ley, Dr Leonard, *Memoirs of a General Medical Practitioner* (via greatyarmouthhistory.com)

Morris, Captain Joseph, *The German Air Raids on Great Britain, 1914-1918* (London: Sampson Low, Marston & Co., 1925, reprinted by The Naval & Military Press, 1993)

Peel, Mrs C.S., *How We Lived Then* (London: The Bodley Head, 1929)

Poolman, Kenneth, *Zeppelins Over England* (London: Evans Brothers, 1960)

Robinson, Douglas H., *The Zeppelin in Combat* (Henley-on-Thames: G.T. Foulis & Co., 1962)

Preston Muddock, J.E. (Dick Donovan) *"All Clear" A Brief Record of the Work of the London Special Constabulary 1914-1919* (London: Everett & Co, 1920)

Rimmel, Raymond Laurence, *The Airship VC* (Buckinghamshire, Aston Publications, 1989)

- *Zeppelin! A battle for war supremacy in World War I*, (London: Conway Maritime Press, 1984)

- *Zeppelin Volumes One and Two, and Zeppelins at War! 1914-1915* (2006, 2008 and 2014); - *The Last Flight of The L48, The Last Flight of The L32; The Last Flight of The L31* (2006, 2016 and 2016) (all Berkhamsted: Albatross Productions Ltd)

Simpson, Alan, *Air Raids on South-West Essex in the Great War* (Barnsley: Pen & Sword Aviation, 2015)

Southall, Robert, *Take Me Back to Dear Old Blighty: The First World War through the eyes of the Heraldic China Manufacturers* (Horndean: Milestone Publications, 1982)

Taylor, James, *Pack Up Your Troubles. How Humorous Postcards Helped Win World War I* (London: Bloomsbury, 2016)

Van Emden, Richard and Humphries, Steve, *All Quiet on the Home Front An Oral History of Life in Britain during the First World War* (London: Headline, 2004)

Wyatt, R.J., *Death From The Skies – The Zeppelin Raids Over Norfolk 19 January 1915* (Norwich: Gliddon Books, 1990)

Websites:

www.iancastlezeppelin.co.uk Ian Castle's aim is to provide details of every airship and aeroplane raid on Britain during the First World War. It is building into an invaluable resource for historians and researchers.

www.airshipsonline.com The website for the Airship Heritage Trust, where you will find an extensive history relating to all of the British Airships from 1900 to the present day.

Acknowledgements

When I finally took the decision to give talks on the subject of First World War Zeppelin raids in 2013, I wanted these to be illustrated, as far as possible, with postcards and ephemera from my own collection. Audiences particularly enjoyed the comic postcards and I had the idea of expanding the idea into a book based on the collection. While I dabbled with various formats, it was only in the last couple of years that things finally fell into place and I would take this opportunity to express my gratitude to those people who have assisted and encouraged me over the last few years.

In particular, I would like to give my sincere thanks to Ian Castle, a fine writer, engaging speaker and diligent researcher on the 'First Blitz'. His help and suggestions have been invaluable. I must also thank Doctor Giles Camplin of the Airship Heritage Trust, as his boundless energy and enthusiasm with regard to the history and future of airships have been an inspiration. Thanks also go to Mick Forsyth, for assisting with the German translations and his guidance, and to the rest of the Great War Forum London 'Pals' for their support. I would also like to thank Brian Lund and James Taylor for their input and ideas, and Ray Rimmel for his encyclopedic knowledge of William Leefe Robinson and the many books he has written on the Zeppelin at war.

It would be remiss of me not to mention the partners and staff of David Rubin & Partners where I have worked for coming up on eighteen eventful years. Thank you for allowing me the time to indulge my passion for Zeppelins and the First World War in general. Finally, the biggest thank you goes to my parents for instilling in me a love of collecting, history and the finer things in life.

David Marks,

November 2016